Furgang, Kathy

Leonardo DiCaprio: environmental
champion

CELEBRITY ACTIVISTS™

LEONARDO DICAPRIO

ENVIRONMENTAL CHAMPION

ROSEN
PUBLISHING®

New York

**KATHY FURGANG AND
ADAM FURGANG**

Dedicated to the earth. May it stay healthy
for our children and generations beyond.

Published in 2009 by The Rosen Publishing Group, Inc.
29 East 21st Street, New York, NY 10010
www.rosenpublishing.com

First Edition

Library of Congress Cataloging-in-Publication Data

Furgang, Kathy.
Leonardo DiCaprio: environmental champion / Kathy and Adam Furgang.
    p. cm.—(Celebrity activists)
Includes bibliographical references and index.
ISBN-13: 978-1-4042-1764-5 (library binding)
1. DiCaprio, Leonardo. 2. Environmentalists—United States—Biography. 3. Green movement—United States. I. Furgang, Adam. II. Title.
GE56.D53F87 2009
333.72092—dc22

                                                                    2007040190

Manufactured in Malaysia

On the cover: Inset: Leonardo DiCaprio. Background: Heavy traffic in Los Angeles, California.

CONTENTS

When you think of the most
famous actors of our time,
just a handful come to mind.
Leonardo DiCaprio is one of those
actors. At a young age, he achieved a
level of success most actors never reach
during their whole careers. DiCaprio
has worked with other talented and
famous actors, such as Robert DeNiro,
Jack Nicholson, and Tom Hanks. He
has also worked with some of
Hollywood's biggest and most famous
film directors, including Martin Scorsese
and James Cameron. DiCaprio is
already a three-time Academy Award
nominee, and he won a Golden Globe
Award for Best Actor for his portrayal

Leonardo DiCaprio in 2007 at the 79th Annual Academy Awards, held at the Kodak Theatre in Hollywood, California. He was nominated for Best Actor for *Blood Diamond*.

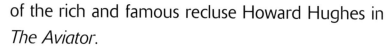

of the rich and famous recluse Howard Hughes in
The Aviator.

Leonardo Wilhelm DiCaprio was born on
November 11, 1974, in Los Angeles, California.
Before he was even born, his parents, Irmelin and
George, had decided to name their baby after the
great Renaissance painter Leonardo da Vinci. As the
story goes, a pregnant Irmelin was looking at a
painting by the artist when her little baby moved
inside her. She decided right there that if the baby
was a boy she would call him Leonardo.

When DiCaprio was a child, life was not ideal. He
lived in a rundown area of Los Angeles, just north of
Hollywood Boulevard, and before he was a year old,
his parents had separated. Despite the split, Irmelin
and George got along and made sure Leonardo
spent time with both of them. The boy lived with his
mother but also spent a lot of time at his father's
house. As a result, young Leonardo was able to
remain close with both of his parents.

DiCaprio was first inspired to be an actor when he
saw his stepbrother, Adam Starr, appear in television
commercials. Adam was the son of George DiCaprio

and his second wife. After Leonardo spent some time doing his own commercials and appearing in small roles on television shows, he was cast in the television version of the film *Parenthood*.

DiCaprio also landed a part on the popular television series *Growing Pains* during its final season. He played a homeless boy named Luke Brower. It was during this time that he had his first film role, in the movie *Critters 3*.

DiCaprio's first critical acclaim came shortly after this, in 1993, for his portrayal of Toby in *This Boy's Life*. The film was based on the childhood of author Tobias Wolfe. In it, DiCaprio acted alongside Robert DeNiro and Ellen Barkin. DiCaprio was only nineteen years old when the film was released. Also in 1993, he costarred in the popular film *What's Eating Gilbert Grape*. DiCaprio played Arnie, the mentally handicapped younger brother of Gilbert Grape, played by Johnny Depp.

DiCaprio then went on to play Jim Carroll in *The Basketball Diaries*, a film about the young poet's struggle with drug addiction. His riveting performance received critical acclaim. Janet Maslin of the *New*

York Times even compared him to James Dean, a teen heartthrob and highly regarded actor from the 1950s. DiCaprio's acting career was well on its way.

In 1997, DiCaprio went on to star in *Titanic*, James Cameron's epic film about the ill-fated maiden voyage of the famous RMS *Titanic*, a luxury liner that sank after hitting an iceberg. *Titanic* was a huge success and went on to break every box-office record at the time. As of 2007, it was still the all-time highest grossing film worldwide, having earned almost $2 billion. After the success of *Titanic*, DiCaprio shot to superstar status worldwide.

More recently, DiCaprio partnered with Martin Scorsese for three films: *Gangs of New York*, *The Aviator*, and *The Departed*. DiCaprio received an Academy Award nomination for Best Actor for his role in *The Aviator*, and he won a Golden Globe Award for Best Actor that year for the same role.

In the 2006 film *Blood Diamond*, DiCaprio starred as a diamond smuggler in West Africa's war-torn Sierra Leone. For that role, he received another Academy Award nomination for Best Actor.

In addition to all his accomplishments as an actor, Leonardo DiCaprio has branched out into another

area that he feels passionate about—environmental activism. His film *The 11th Hour* is a documentary about the current neglected state of our planet. In *The 11th Hour*, DiCaprio and a host of environmental experts explain how we need to change our current bad habits and bad choices to live more in harmony with nature.

Leonardo DiCaprio has used his fame to bring more awareness to an important topic. His actions have helped to make people more aware of environmental issues and have brought attention to things we can do to treat the environment in a more responsible way.

CHAPTER ONE

Environmentalism 101

M any think that in order to be an environmentalist, one must be either a scientist or an expert on the subject. In reality, however, it is not necessary to be an expert to be considered an environmentalist. The goal of environmentalism is to be informed about the natural world around you. In an interview on ABC's *Nightline* on August 10, 2007, Leonardo DiCaprio admitted that he is not an environmental expert. While on the show, DiCaprio deferred to environmental expert Kenny Ausubel, who helped to answer scientific questions and discuss the important issues at hand.

DiCaprio's main goal as a high-profile environmentalist is to raise awareness of important issues and to help bring about change. Even as early as 2000, DiCaprio was very much in the public eye with his environmentalist message. That year, he was the chairperson of the Earth Day celebrations in Washington, D.C. In his opening speech, he explained, "Ever since I was a little kid, environmental issues have sparked my interest." He is now even more committed to the environmental movement. He is widely recognized as a spokesman for change, raising awareness of how humans have negatively altered and impacted our environment, and how we can improve the state of it. Part of his goal has been to bring focus to these important topics, while at the same time not putting himself and his fame too much in the spotlight. He also wants to communicate to people how we all can help in making change possible.

What Are Fossil Fuels?

In order to understand DiCaprio's message about preserving the environment, we must first understand the basics of how the environment works and how our actions may negatively impact it. The planet

What Is Environmentalism?

"Environmentalism" is a term used to describe the actions and concerns of those who protect and improve the environment. It involves an active participation in reducing the effects of pollution and other problems that affect our ecosystems. Scientists and ecologists research the effects that humans have on their environments. Then regular people can use this information to make changes in the way they live. Taking intelligent steps to alter our negative impact on the planet and learning to live in harmony with nature are the primary goals of the environmental movement. People who act purposefully on such beliefs are called environmental activists.

Earth is a natural, self-sustaining system. Life on Earth gets energy from the sun, the star our planet orbits. Plants use a process called photosynthesis to convert the sun's energy, or solar energy, into a form of energy they can use. In turn, many animals, including humans, then eat plants to gather food energy for themselves. Other animals, humans included, may eat the plant-eating animals, adding more links to the food chain that begins with solar energy.

This power plant burns coal, a fossil fuel. Burning fossil fuels adds carbon dioxide to the air, contributing to global warming.

To aid in photosynthesis, plants take in the gas carbon dioxide, or CO_2. They then give off oxygen as a waste byproduct of this process. Animals, in turn, breathe in oxygen from the atmosphere and give off carbon dioxide as a waste product. This is a symbiotic system in which plants and animals mutually benefit. We need the oxygen in the air, and plants need the carbon dioxide in the air.

During much of the earth's history, solar energy has been converted by this process into plant or animal tissue—organic matter. When plants and animals die, their remains stay on the earth's surface and begin to decay. This decaying matter is eventually buried under more and more layered deposits of earth. Over millions of years, pressure and heat slowly turn some of the organic matter into oil or coal, depending on its location. In this way, oil and coal are remains of the earth's past history. Because they form much like fossils do, they are called fossil fuels.

Ten thousand years ago, there were only about ten million people on the earth. Two thousand years ago, our numbers grew to nearly three hundred million people. And today, the worldwide population has skyrocketed to more than six and a half billion. In our recent history, humans learned to mine oil and coal and burn them as a source of energy. This discovery has undoubtedly helped civilization to progress. Thanks to the Industrial Revolution and the burning of fossil fuels, we now have the modern conveniences that we couldn't live without. But the world has changed around us. Instead of helping the progress of the human race, fossil fuels have begun to harm us.

How? In just the last 150 years or so, humans have burned such vast amounts of fossil fuels that the additional carbon dioxide waste gases in the earth's atmosphere have begun to change the climate of our planet. Today, coal is used to produce electricity everywhere, and oil is the primary source for energy around the world. Oil is very portable and can easily be shipped around the globe and then refined into higher-energy fuels such as gasoline or diesel fuel. Most of the cars we drive today run on fossil fuels. Take a look at any busy highway and you will be able to see the scope of the problem we are facing.

The Greenhouse Effect

The increased CO_2 in the atmosphere is dangerous because it accelerates the earth's natural greenhouse effect. In a real greenhouse, a layer of glass traps heat generated by the sun's rays to maintain an environment that helps plants grow better. The earth's greenhouse effect works in a similar way, on a huge scale. Energy from sunlight (infrared radiation)

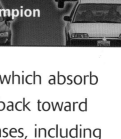

heats up the earth and the oceans, which absorb some of the heat and reflect some back toward space. In the earth's atmosphere, gases, including water vapor, carbon dioxide, methane, ozone, and others, trap this heat, causing the atmosphere to become warmer.

A certain amount of greenhouse effect occurs naturally on the earth. In fact, without the greenhouse effect, life as we know it would not be possible here. Still, this warming could possibly increase beyond what is tolerable for humans and other plants and animals. Imagine being trapped inside a room that is filling with a toxic gas. The earth is experiencing something similar, with increasing levels of carbon dioxide in the atmosphere. This is what is known as the enhanced greenhouse effect. For many scientists today, their greatest concern is an enhanced greenhouse effect that causes atmospheric temperatures to increase beyond the small window of what is tolerable or acceptable.

What Is Global Warming?

Global warming, as the term is meant most often today, is the gradual increase in the temperature of the earth's surface and near atmosphere due to the enhanced greenhouse effect. The human effect on the earth's atmosphere is only a recent occurrence, as far as the history of the planet is concerned. After all, the earth is about four and a half billion years old. Scientists think there have been numerous global warming and cooling periods, which occurred independent of human involvement. (The last great ice age ended around ten thousand years ago, when there were only ten million people on the earth.) These natural, global changes are caused by various geological effects, the natural water cycle, the intensity of the sun's rays, and the positioning of the earth in relation to the sun, among other things.

In an interview with *National Geographic Kids*, DiCaprio warns that human-caused global warming is "changing the climate of our planet. And in doing so, global warming is changing our way of life all around the planet." He goes on to say that his work with environmental organizations has taught him that "scientists have gathered a lot of evidence showing that one of the reasons behind the increase in Earth's temperatures is an increased amount of

Global Warming Fast Facts

- Global warming is being felt around the world, with average temperatures having climbed 1.4 degrees Fahrenheit (0.8 degrees Celsius) since 1880.
- According to several climate studies, the last two decades of the twentieth century were the hottest in four hundred years.
- Human activity is putting carbon dioxide into the atmosphere faster than plants and the oceans can absorb it.
- The United States represents only 5 percent of the world's population but consumes 25 percent of the world's oil and energy.
- Polar bears that depend on ice to hunt for food have been threatened by decreasing ice in recent years.
- Many governments around the world have acknowledged global warming as a serious prob-lem. An international agreement called the Kyoto Protocol states by how much each country has agreed to decrease its greenhouse gas emissions.
- Scientists warn that increasing global temperatures are contributing to more extreme weather con-ditions. These may result in more frequent and intense wildfires, destructive tropical storms, and severe droughts.

carbon dioxide emissions from human activities like driving cars and powering factories."

With data collected from various sources, scientists have determined that the surface temperature of the earth has increased by more than one degree Fahrenheit (0.6 degrees Celsius) over the last one hundred years. That is enough to cause environmental problems for humans around the globe.

One adverse climate change that can occur from hotter atmospheric temperatures is a rise in sea level. This can result when glaciers and ice caps in polar regions melt due to the increased atmospheric temperature. Of all the earth's freshwater, nearly 70 percent of it is found in ice and glaciers. This ice is mostly located around the colder polar regions of the earth, which receive little direct sunlight. The polar ice caps are slowly melting. Over time, this melting raises the level of the oceans. A sea level rise of only a few feet would negatively affect many large urban centers and coastal communities worldwide.

What Is a Carbon Footprint?

"Carbon footprint" is the term used to describe the quantity of greenhouse gases emitted by humans as a result of their various activities. A carbon footprint is measured in units of carbon dioxide. The measurement is based on things like the type of energy used to run your home, the amount and method of your travel, and the amount of electricity used in your home. Someone who emits a lot of carbon dioxide as part of his or her activities would be described as having a larger carbon footprint than someone whose activities produce less carbon dioxide emissions.

In our daily lives, almost all of us add to the overall carbon footprint. Carbon emissions are produced whenever we drive a car, use public transportation,

Russell Glacier in Greenland shows the effects of global warming. The glacier's ice caps are melting, and its thick ice sheets are retreating.

and heat or cool our homes. Producing the foods we eat also contributes to a carbon footprint. Products like toys, clothes, books, and other common items also generate a carbon footprint when they are manufactured, shipped, and then delivered to consumers. By buying a product, you contribute to the overall demand for that product and the need for it to be manufactured.

In order to improve the state of our environment and reduce greenhouse gas emissions, we can all take steps to reduce our carbon footprint. Manufacturing corporations can help by, for example, making more energy-efficient appliances and cars. Consumers can help by educating themselves and choosing to buy these more efficient appliances and cars. Individuals can take many simple steps, such as turning off lights when they are not being used, taking public transportation, recycling, and just using and making do with less of something. Many people bring their own reuseable bags to grocery stores in order to curb the manufacture of paper and plastic bags.

For a high-profile celebrity like Leonardo DiCaprio, reducing one's carbon footprint is not easy. Celebrities are often criticized in the media for not practicing what they preach. While DiCaprio does not lead an average American life, he has taken many steps to reduce his carbon footprint and bring his lifestyle more in harmony with the environment.

In an interview on ABC's *Nightline*, DiCaprio spoke briefly about his home, which he said was constructed to be eco-friendly. It has solar panels, proper insulation, and air and water filtration systems. In addition, DiCaprio said he flies on commercial airlines rather than private jets whenever possible, to prevent unnecessary amounts of carbon dioxide emissions. No one can be perfect, however. In the interview, he admitted that he does occasionally fly on private jets when film industry timetables make it impractical for him to fly commercial. He also noted that if hybrid jets did exist, he would be using them. A hybrid vehicle is one that is powered in more than one way. For example, a hybrid car may run on both a gasoline engine and an electric motor. This saves on gasoline and therefore cuts down in carbon dioxide emissions. Unfortunately, reliable hybrid aircraft have not yet been produced.

What Is Sustainable Energy?

As noted, today, most of the energy we consume comes from fossil fuels such as oil, coal, and natural gas. All of these fuels when burned emit some amount of carbon dioxide into the earth's atmosphere, which contributes to global warming. Also, fossil fuels are nonrenewable energy sources, meaning that there is a finite amount of them available to us. It takes millions of years for coal and oil to form, and we are using these resources faster than they are being created in nature. So, once resources such as oil and coal run out, they are gone forever. In addition to the damage caused to the atmosphere from burning these resources, mining them harms the land. Surface vegetation must be destroyed to get to the resources, and the mining process often ruins water supplies with poisonous runoff. Environmentalists say that we can no longer be dependent on nonrenewable energy sources that harm the environment, and they urge that we change sooner rather than later.

Unlike nonrenewable fossil fuels, sustainable energy sources will not run out and will have little

This wind farm in Liverpool Bay, England, is made up of twenty-five wind turbines. This sustainable source of electricity can power about 80,000 homes.

negative impact on the environment. Renewable or sustainable energy sources that use nature's processes to generate power are available to us today. Wind energy, for example, is generated by the endless natural movement of air in the earth's atmosphere. Solar energy comes from the sun, which will continue to burn for several billion years. Geothermal energy comes from heat produced by natural processes inside the earth. Hydroelectric

and tidal energy are generated by the natural movement of water.

For obvious reasons, sustainable energy helps to stem the use of carbon-emitting fossil fuels. In the United States and throughout the world, steps are being taken to replace fossil fuels with sustainable energy sources. Unfortunately, much of modern society is still based on the old systems. It will be difficult to rebuild our world based on new energy sources, but these important changes must be made, one step at a time.

One of Leonardo DiCaprio's more recent projects stresses the importance of renewable energy. DiCaprio is teaming with Discovery Communications to help the people of Greensburg, Kansas, a small town of 1,500 people that was destroyed by a tornado on May 4, 2007. DiCaprio's plan is to rebuild Greensburg as an eco-friendly town, using sustainable energy sources. The project, which will be filmed and turned into a reality show, will showcase sustainable energy for all of America to see. (See sidebar on page 89 for more details about the project.)

CHAPTER TWO

Becoming an Environmentalist

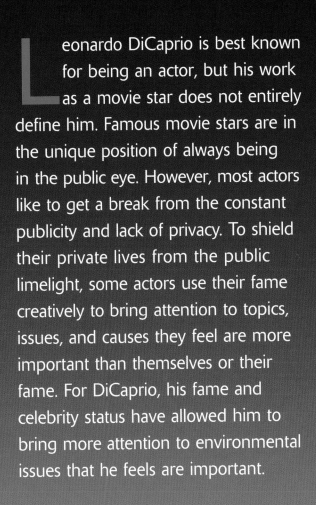

Leonardo DiCaprio is best known for being an actor, but his work as a movie star does not entirely define him. Famous movie stars are in the unique position of always being in the public eye. However, most actors like to get a break from the constant publicity and lack of privacy. To shield their private lives from the public limelight, some actors use their fame creatively to bring attention to topics, issues, and causes they feel are more important than themselves or their fame. For DiCaprio, his fame and celebrity status have allowed him to bring more attention to environmental issues that he feels are important.

Here, former U.S. vice president Al Gore is shown narrating *An Inconvenient Truth*. In 2006, the documentary began raising awareness in America about the problem of global warming.

Leonardo's Green Roots

In a 2007 interview, a Reuters news service reporter asked DiCaprio why he became involved in environmental issues. "It goes back to my childhood," the actor responded, "and came from watching documentaries about the rainforest and the loss of habitats and species. After that *Titanic* movie, I wanted to become more involved. There was a lot of attention on me, and I wanted to focus on something meaningful to me."

When asked about global warming and why that in particular was something that appealed to him as an area of focus, DiCaprio told the interviewer, "It was a visit to the White House. The vice president at the time, Al Gore, sat me down for an hour and drew out a map of what exactly global warming was, and how he felt it was the greatest challenge of the next millennium. Since then—that was the late 1990s—I've become an activist."

Different actors have different groups of fans. After his starring role in *Titanic*, the handsome DiCaprio became very popular with younger audiences. Knowing this, he used his fame to appeal to young people specifically. He urged them directly to educate

What Does It Mean to Be Green?

"Green" is a term used to describe people, groups, products, or items that are environmentally conscious. Products that use recycled paper can be seen as green. People who strive to reduce their carbon footprint by using less energy in their daily activities can be considered green. Reusing empty plastic containers rather than discarding them is a good way to start "thinking green." Other simple measures one can take include walking or biking instead of driving, turning off the air conditioner, using a hand-powered lawn mower, catching rainwater from gutters to use in the garden on a dry day, or buying foods and other products that are produced in environmentally conscious ways. All of these small efforts add up, and collectively, they help. More ambitious green efforts include planting trees or a vegetable garden, using solar or wind energy to heat or power one's home, and buying a hybrid car, which uses less gasoline.

themselves about topics that he felt were important for the future of the planet and to future generations. But his alignment with Hollywood and young people created some of its own challenges in his early years as a celebrity activist.

The Beach

The controversy surrounding DiCaprio's film *The Beach* provides a good example of why it is not easy to bring an environmental message to the public while also being a popular Hollywood actor. In 1999, filming began on *The Beach*, a movie based on the book of the same name by Alex Garland. DiCaprio starred in the story of Richard, a disenchanted young

This photo, taken in January 1999, shows Maya Bay, Thailand, just before filming began on *The Beach*.

American who travels to Thailand in search of something new. After coming across a map showing directions to a small, obscure island, Richard and two other travelers set out to find the island and the mysterious utopian community that has supposedly been established there. In the book, the community is located near an idyllic beach, tucked away in a small bay and shielded from view by sheer cliffs on all sides.

The actual beach that was used for filming was on Maya Bay, located within a national park on Phi Phi Island in Thailand. The studio producing the movie, 20th Century Fox, secured permission from Thai officials to seal off the beach from public use for six weeks during filming. Controversy began almost instantly, with a suit filed against 20th Century Fox and the Thai officials who permitted filming there. Filming was allowed, with the case pending in Thai courts, and several protests were staged as the filming began.

The actual location in Thailand was beautiful, but it did not quite fit the book's description of the tropical paradise. So, in order to create the look and feel the film producers wanted, the beach was altered, and native plants were uprooted and moved to greenhouses for the duration of the filming. Many of the plants did not survive. In addition, coconut trees were brought in and planted to suit the film's visual requirements.

When reports surfaced that the dunes had been damaged during filming, film producer Andrew Macdonald said that tropical storms, not the alterations made by the film crew, had damaged the dunes. In a BBC News article, published January 18, 1999, Macdonald said, "We honestly believe we are making some temporary changes to the environment but it will not damage it in the long run."

During this period, DiCaprio became directly involved in helping to restore the beach to its original state. The actor was made aware of the controversy and worked with the Natural Resources Defense Council and the World Conservation Union to try to solve the problem. In a letter to the World Conservation Union, he wrote, "I am personally committed to resolving the controversy over *The Beach* in a manner that serves to protect the environment of Maya Bay and Thailand." DiCaprio hoped his involvement would "serve as a model for future

In May 2004, Leonardo DiCaprio spoke at an event in Los Angeles that raised more than $2 million for the Natural Resources Defense Council (NRDC).

partnerships between the motion picture industry and conservation organizations."

Eventually, the Thai citizens moved forward with their legal case against 20th Century Fox as well as the many Thai government officials who may have abused their power by allowing the film crews to alter a national park. It was argued that the alterations were unlawful and that the reconstruction efforts to restore the beach to its original state failed, permanently altering the beach's ecosystem. The incident certainly did not enhance DiCaprio's image as a spokesman for environmental protection. At the end of 2007, the case was still being argued in civil court.

Earth Day 2000

Leonardo DiCaprio was the chairman of Earth Day 2000 celebrations in Washington, D.C. To bring attention to the event and to the issue of the environment, he conducted an interview with then president Bill Clinton for an ABC special.

Even before the interview was to air on April 22, many in the media commented that DiCaprio's reputation as a teen heartthrob detracted from the serious messages he wished to communicate. In a

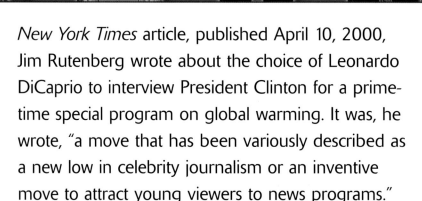

New York Times article, published April 10, 2000,
Jim Rutenberg wrote about the choice of Leonardo
DiCaprio to interview President Clinton for a prime-
time special program on global warming. It was, he
wrote, "a move that has been variously described as
a new low in celebrity journalism or an inventive
move to attract young viewers to news programs."

However, in defense of his choice, then president
of ABC News David Westin responded, "If we don't
add a younger audience, sooner or later our audience
will die."

In a later *New York Times* article written by Gregg
Easterbrook, the criticism was more cutting and
harsh. The article, published April 15, 2000, opened
sarcastically: "Fourteen-year-old girls everywhere can
breathe now that ABC News has decided to go
ahead and broadcast its Earth Day special in which
Leonardo DiCaprio, crusading journalist, questions
President Clinton about global warming. Personally,
I know I'll be waiting for his question on the latest
Intergovernmental Panel on Climate Change science-
assessment revisions, especially as they apply to new
studies on ocean-current fluid dynamics when

compared to the watts-per-square-foot forcing of anthropogenic gases, and how this will affect the Kyoto Annex I plans for joint implementation of carbon sequestration."

Easterbrook continued, "Be these things as they may, ABC asserts that it is sending a teen heartthrob to interview the president about global warming in order to raise public awareness of the issue. But it's fair to suppose that one reason public concern over the greenhouse effect is low is exactly that Hollywood is on the case. When the networks and movie studios treat global warming as a subject so trifling, it can be safely passed off from serious discussion to glam events hosted by celebrities."

The fact that ABC had allowed a young actor, not a professional journalist, to conduct the interview actually served to draw attention away from the environmental concerns that DiCaprio was working hard to bring into the public eye. In the end, only about three minutes of the twenty-minute interview aired during the ABC Earth Day Special, although the White House eventually released the full transcript of the interview.

Interview with President Clinton:
Planet Earth 2000

Like Leonardo DiCaprio, President Bill Clinton is not an expert on the environment and global warming. However, with Al Gore as his vice president, Clinton was certainly well read on the issue and had given it a lot of thought before sitting down to be interviewed in front of a national television audience. In the interview, DiCaprio asked the president why the issue of global warming is not a front-page issue. Knowing now how prominent global warming is in our national consciousness, it's clear that the times have changed since 2000.

DiCaprio: Why do you think this issue is so constantly overlooked, and why do you think people don't take it seriously enough? And for you, is it as important as something like health care or education?

President Clinton: Oh, yes, over the long run, it's one of the two or three major issues facing the world over the next thirty years. I think it's because it takes a long time for the climate to change in a way that people feel it, and because it seems sort of abstract now. That's why I think it's important that programs like this are aired, and people like you—not politicians or scientific experts, but citizens—express their concern.

And then it's important that citizens know that it ought to be an issue—it ought to be a voting issue at election time. And I don't say this in a hateful way, it's just that people need to tell the politicians and the candidates they care about this, they want action. But our citizens need to follow the lead of a lot of our religious groups and other civic groups in actually doing things themselves.

Right now, if the American people knew all the options that are available to them and understood the economics, we could do much better. And, of course, if my plan were to pass the Congress and we were to give the tax breaks to consumers and manufacturers of these products and technologies, we could do it even faster.

Facing Critics

The world news we hear every day can often be confusing and contradictory. One day you might read about dramatic changes happening to our environment as a result of human activity, and then

Pledge of Allegiance to American Energy Independen

I hereby declare my pledge of allegiance to America's independence from
nation's economically and environmentally damaging reliance on foreign
domestic oil, and fossil fuels.

In order to promote the long-term health of the economy and the efficient
of my taxpayer dollars, I call upon my elected officials to pass legislation
improves fuel efficiency standards and increases investment in renewable
energy. Our nation and world needs a future powered by clean energy - inclu
solar, wind and hydrogen from renewable sources - not coal and nuclear p

I urge our legislative   nd that U.S. automakers increase rese
develop-ment and ma   ic, hybrid and fuel cell vehicles. I fu
call upon our electe   g state and municipal government
agencies, to purcha   vehicles, renewable energy, and gre
building technolog

I here   nt to improve my own automobile's fu
                  ce. I also will seek out new car purch
                  or utilize alternative fuel technology,
                  ome and, where possible, purchase solar

        being of the environment, and the security of ou
        future generations.

www.globalgreen.org

GLOBAL GREEN USA

GLOBAL

During the 2004 Green Cross Millennium Awards presented by Global
Green USA, Leonardo DiCaprio signs the "Pledge of Allegiance to
American Energy Independence."

the next day you might see a television news report with a contrary message, saying that the future is not as bleak as others are making it seem. Which side is telling the truth?

The short answer is that most sources agree that accelerated climate change is occurring and can most likely be attributed to humans burning fossil fuels. However, what may happen as a result of this warming is less clear, since it involves predictions based on uncertain data and computer models. The United States Environmental Protection Agency's Web site (http://www.epa.gov) states, "Scientists are certain that human activities are changing the composition of the atmosphere, and that increasing the concentration of greenhouse gases will change the planet's climate. But they are not sure by how much it will change, at what rate it will change, or what the exact effects will be."

On the same Web site, a section specifically for kids states, "A warmer Earth may lead to changes in rainfall patterns, a rise in sea level, and a wide range of impacts on plants, wildlife, and humans."

For Leonardo DiCaprio, the issue of global warming goes beyond environmental concerns into the area of human rights. In a Copley News Service interview from August 24, 2007, DiCaprio addressed questions about the environment. When asked about skeptics who do not believe that our energy consumption is affecting the environment, DiCaprio said, "My response to that has always been, how could we as a country not be for wanting to be energy independent and not reliant on foreign oil? If you don't believe in the overwhelming scientific community that is in agreement that mankind is playing a major role in this, how could we not want cleaner air, cleaner water? These are fundamental human rights issues. So I think it crosses political boundaries in a huge way. And that's my big statement in response to the skeptics."

In the same article, DiCaprio was asked how he felt about those media critics who "nitpick" about his personal consumption. "Well," the actor answered, "I think it's unfortunate that in a lot of media debates about this issue we aren't looking at the bigger picture. It becomes this constant rhetoric and this constant argument about the specifics of what we do personally. This is my new statement after making this movie [*The 11th Hour*] and listening to experts:

We all can do only so much, considering the types of lifestyles that we have. And the environmental movement isn't about telling people how to live or pushing our viewpoints on others. It's about being more aware of these global forces that are out there and being more aware next time you buy something. And being more aware next time you vote for someone."

Ultimately, there is no end to the contradictory information out there regarding the environment. But each one of us can still make changes that we feel certain are helping rather than hurting the environment. Many of these changes are easy to do and will help reduce waste at home, give us a chance to get more exercise, and save us money. How can anyone argue with those results?

CHAPTER THREE

The Leonardo DiCaprio Foundation

A fter all the ups and downs, all the bad press surrounding *The Beach*, and all the criticism he received for his interview with President Bill Clinton, Leonardo DiCaprio stuck it out and continued to work toward raising awareness of environmental issues worldwide. A major step in raising DiCaprio's environmentalist profile came in 1998, when he started the Leonardo DiCaprio Foundation. Since its founding, DiCaprio's foundation has helped to bring awareness to many environmental concerns through its association with various other organizations, including the International Fund for Animal Welfare, *National Geographic*

Kids, the Natural Resources Defense Council, and Global Green USA. DiCaprio is now on the boards of directors of Global Green USA and the Natural Resources Defense Council. As a board member, he has input into the ways in which the organizations go about their missions of increasing environmental protection and raising awareness. In addition to his behind-the-scenes work, DiCaprio has also given many speeches about the environment to promote awareness, responsibility, and change for a more eco-friendly future.

In 2001, DiCaprio received the Martin Litton Environmental Warrior Award from Environment Now, a nonprofit foundation dedicated to protecting and restoring the environment of California. In 2003, the actor received the Celebrity for the Environment Award from Star Eco Station, an environmental education and wildlife rescue foundation with centers in Sacramento and Los Angeles, California. Also in 2003, DiCaprio received the Entertainment Industry Environmental Leadership Award from Global Green USA, the United States affiliate of Green Cross International, an organization dedicated to promoting the use of sustainable energy around the world.

DiCaprio spoke at a May 2004 Natural Resources Defense Council benefit called "Earth to L.A.!—The Greatest Show on Earth."

At his acceptance speech for his award from Global Green, DiCaprio pointed out that our oil-based industrial society presently depends on nonrenewable resources. Of our thirst for oil, he commented, "It requires relentless probing into vast reaches of pristine land, sacrificing vital bioregions and irreplaceable cultures. The possibility of catastrophic climate change is substantially increased by the 40 million barrels of oil burned every day by vehicles." And in a call to arms, he continued, "We must all move shoulder to shoulder in a unified front to show [the Bush] administration that the true majority of people are willing to vote for a cleaner environment and won't back down."

Get Informed

As an environmentalist, Leonardo DiCaprio makes it clear that he thinks getting informed is the first step on the road to changing our habits to create a cleaner future for the earth. On October 19, 2004, DiCaprio gave a speech at Case Western University in Cleveland, Ohio, in which he said, "You don't have to be a lawmaker, scientist, or in the White House to take action to protect the environment. Reduce your own impact on the environment in your daily lives. Most importantly, get educated about local, state, and national politicians and their environmental policies." He added, "Individual action is critically important, as we can make decisions in our daily lives that can change the planet little by little."

The DiCaprio Foundation Web site has an entire section dedicated to getting informed. Here is the link: http://www.leonardodicaprio.org/getinformed.

In his efforts to get his environmental message out to the masses, DiCaprio has also appeared on many television news and talk shows, including *The Oprah Winfrey Show*, *Nightline*, and *The Early Show*. When DiCaprio appeared on *The Oprah Winfrey*

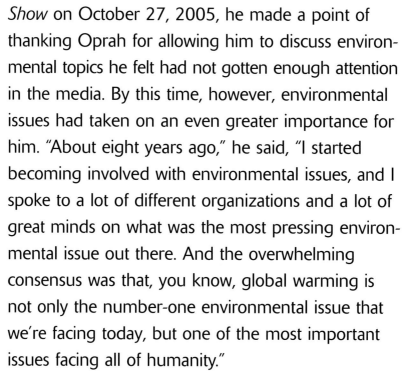

Show on October 27, 2005, he made a point of thanking Oprah for allowing him to discuss environmental topics he felt had not gotten enough attention in the media. By this time, however, environmental issues had taken on an even greater importance for him. "About eight years ago," he said, "I started becoming involved with environmental issues, and I spoke to a lot of different organizations and a lot of great minds on what was the most pressing environmental issue out there. And the overwhelming consensus was that, you know, global warming is not only the number-one environmental issue that we're facing today, but one of the most important issues facing all of humanity."

The show ended with a discussion of various things people can do to help reduce the consumption of carbon-based fuels. One of the things mentioned was to switch to more energy-efficient lightbulbs, such as compact fluorescent bulbs. Although they cost a bit more, they use much less electricity over the life of the bulb than ordinary ones, making them more cost-efficient.

The Leonardo DiCaprio Foundation Web site (http://www.leonardodicaprio.org), called "Eco-Site,"

is an easy way for people to get involved with the environment. At the site, you will find headings such as "What's Important," "What You Can Do," and "Get Informed." The site was created to draw more attention to environmental issues by using DiCaprio's name and high profile as a way to attract readers. People who wish to get involved in environmental issues—or just want to find out more—can go to the site and read articles about the importance of

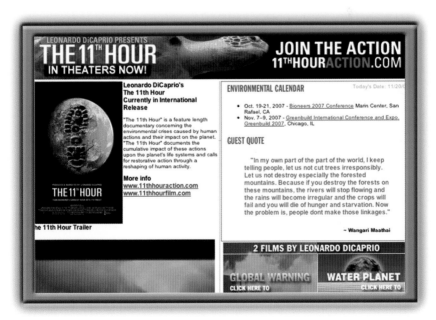

The home page of DiCaprio's Eco-Site (http://www.leonardodicaprio.org) directs you to environmental news, features, and information. It also links to two short environmental Web films narrated by DiCaprio.

sustainable energy and what kinds of alternative energies are available today. You can also read about the ways your lifestyle and everyday purchases contribute to the way humans affect the environment. The site includes a calendar of national events aimed at raising awareness for environmental protection.

Eco-Films

Leonardo DiCaprio's Web site, http://www. leonardodicaprio.org, showcases two short films, *Global Warning* (2003) and *Water Planet* (2005). The films were produced by the Leonardo DiCaprio Foundation and Birken Interactive Studios, Inc. Both films, which last about four to five minutes, are easily accessible on the site. Narrated by DiCaprio, they are fast-paced, eye-catching cautionary tales, told using still images and text together.

Global Warning was inspired by Thom Hartmann's book *Last Hours of Ancient Sunlight*, published by Three Rivers Press. It focuses on our appetite for oil as a main source of energy. In the film, DiCaprio lays out many alarming facts related to destructive human actions. For instance, he notes that our activity has taken seven hundred billion tons of CO_2 out of the ground and dumped it into the atmosphere. *Global Warning* ends with DiCaprio exhorting, "We must demand a separation between oil and state. We can get off oil and slow down global warming. We can use energy more efficiently and support renewable, clean energy sources—new green technologies that don't burn carbon, like hydrogen fuel cells, wind and solar power. We can vote for leaders who care about protecting your health, the air, and the environment. We can support nonprofits who are making a difference. We can be environmentalists. So get educated, stay educated, so we can think for ourselves. And join the fight to save this unique blue planet for future generations."

The second film, *Water Planet*, focuses on the most important resource we have: water. Within the water cycle, the earth's water is constantly traveling between the earth and the atmosphere through the processes of condensation and evaporation. We can easily see the water cycle at work when rain falls from clouds, and then water from puddles evaporates into the air to form more rain clouds. With the use of text, imagery, and DiCaprio's narration, the film demonstrates the great degree to which life on Earth

Visitors to the Eco-Site can watch a short film called *Global Warning*. It discusses global warming and other problems related to burning fossil fuels.

relies on freshwater, and it points out the various ways our water is being polluted and wasted.

"We are at a crisis point," DiCaprio's narration warns, "but we still have time to turn this around. We can conserve water and not waste it, invest in smart water infrastructure and technologies, increase environmental regulations in polluting industries, tell government leaders to fulfill financial pledges for clean water, insure that water is not treated as a commodity, but most important, we must recognize that access to clean water is a basic human right. And the United Nations should adopt a global treaty for the right to water. Water equals life, there is no separation. By protecting water, we can protect ourselves and this blue planet for future generations."

Biodiversity

Biodiversity is another topic discussed on the Leonardo DiCaprio Foundation Eco-Site. The term "biodiversity" is a combination of the words "biology" and "diversity." Biodiversity is the total variety of living organisms within a specific area, region, or ecosystem. The biodiversity page of the Eco-Site explains that in the last one hundred years, humans have destroyed or altered many natural habitats and caused mass extinction of species, dramatically decreasing biodiversity within these ecosystems. More than a dozen Web sites and organizations that you can get involved with are listed in the site's "Biodiversity" section. Visitors to the site are encouraged to do simple but meaningful things, such as writing to Congress or local government officials to request that funds be allocated to protect lands.

Biodiversity also involves humans living in harmony with nature. We should be aware of where we build and how we use land for our purposes. Since the start of the Industrial Revolution, the earth's natural habitats have suffered from destruction, waste, pollution, and neglect. However, we now have the scientific knowledge and the ability to prevent further catastrophe and damage.

A fundamental change in human behavior will ensure that we are not harming other species that coexist with us. Other changes must also be made with regard to state and local governments as well as

Trees in the Amazon rain forest in Brazil are cut and burned to make room for cattle ranching. The human impact on the ecosystem is devastating.

the corporate world. Laws can be updated to take into account the earth's rich biodiversity while still allowing for progress in a modern and technological society.

Several rotating quotes appear in the "Biodiversity" section of the Eco-Site. They show that living in harmony with nature is not a new idea. In fact, many great thinkers realized the importance of biodiversity. Their words underscore the history and understanding behind this important topic and help to illustrate the need for further positive change:

"For if one link in nature's chain might be lost, another might be lost, until the whole of things will vanish by piecemeal."
—Thomas Jefferson

"If the bee disappeared off the surface of the globe then man would only have four years of life left. No more bees, no more pollination, no more plants, no more animals, no more man."
—Albert Einstein

"If all mankind were to disappear, the world would regenerate back to the rich state of equilibrium that existed ten thousand years ago. If insects were to vanish, the environment would collapse into chaos."

—Edward O. Wilson, the "Father of Biodiversity"

Kids Need to Know

As the saying goes, children are the future. What today's children are taught will determine the direction of our society in the future. The Leonardo DiCaprio Foundation understands this and has set up an entire "Kids" section of its Web site dedicated specifically to educating kids about the growing environmental problems we all face. The information is presented not as dry facts and figures but as something fun and interesting. Kids are encouraged to grow, learn, and have fun while they help protect the planet.

The Leonardo DiCaprio Foundation Web site also has a section where kids can learn about "book stretching." After kids read books recommended on the site, they are encouraged to take what they have

DiCaprio speaks at a Global Green USA news conference in 2005. The event raised awareness about the lack of access to clean water for hundreds of millions of people worldwide.

learned and "stretch" the information, branching out into other activities in their everyday lives. Writing letters, doing art projects, writing in journals, making jewelry, and collecting stamps are just a few of the many suggestions for kids. Other activities, including reading, coloring, word searches, and Web surfing, are also presented on the Eco-Site.

Recycling is another important topic discussed on the site. Recycling is presented as something good

National Geographic Kids

In an interview with *National Geographic Kids* in the Kids section of his Eco-Site, DiCaprio explains why he feels it's important for kids to protect the earth. "Children are our future's resource," the actor notes. "If today's kids learn to make protecting the planet a way of life, it will be a way of life for future generations to protect the Earth." He adds, "When we all work together, even the smallest actions to protect the planet can turn into something huge. Look at it this way: It's no big deal to start taking steps right now to protect the Earth. But it's going to be a really big deal if we don't start now."

for the environment that can also be made into a fun activity. The concept of "reduce, reuse, recycle" is discussed. Items such as envelopes, paper towel tubes, cereal boxes, and plastic bottles are just a few of the everyday items that can be reused to make fun crafts featured on the site. Finally, the site features eco-friendly music and books, as well as links to other important environmental Web sites aimed at young children.

CHAPTER FOUR

The 11th Hour

Sometimes, no matter how much one tries to get an important message across, it may not be understood correctly, heard by enough people, or heard by the right people. Documentary films are a good way to get an important message out to a large number of people. In recent years, many documentaries have helped to raise public awareness of important issues, including environmental protection. Perhaps none of these documentaries has been more notable than Davis Guggenheim's film *An Inconvenient Truth*.

Released in the United States on August 31, 2006, *An Inconvenient Truth* stars former U.S. vice president Al Gore. For much of the film, Gore is shown giving a slideshow to a large group, talking about global warming, the problems surrounding it, and what can be done to help. After raking in huge profits at the box office, *An Inconvenient Truth* went on to win two Academy Awards (Oscars) in 2007, including one for best documentary film. Leonardo DiCaprio was at the Academy Awards that year and appeared on stage with Gore, who thanked the film industry for its response to the climate crisis and singled out DiCaprio for being an important ally in the cause.

A Film for the Environment

Following the success of *An Inconvenient Truth*, DiCaprio worked with sisters Leila Conners Petersen and Nadia Conners to produce his own documentary film about the environment. The women codirected and cowrote the film *The 11th Hour*, which stars DiCaprio as an on- and off-screen narrator. Previously, the trio collaborated on the two short Web films, *Global Warning* and *Water Planet*, that appear on the Leonardo DiCaprio Foundation Eco-Site.

The 11th Hour merges two of DiCaprio's passions: appearing on film and the environment. In the film's press release, put out by Warner Brothers Independent Films, DiCaprio explains how the project came together: "We reached out to independent experts on the front lines of what could be the greatest challenge of our time—the collapse of our planet's ecosystems and our search for solutions to create a sustainable future."

Director Leila Conners Petersen further explains, "We ourselves wanted to understand why humans were on a crash course with nature, and what we had to do to change course."

At the 79th Annual Academy Awards ceremony in 2007, Al Gore and DiCaprio spoke about the environment. Gore was honored for the documentary *An Inconvenient Truth.*

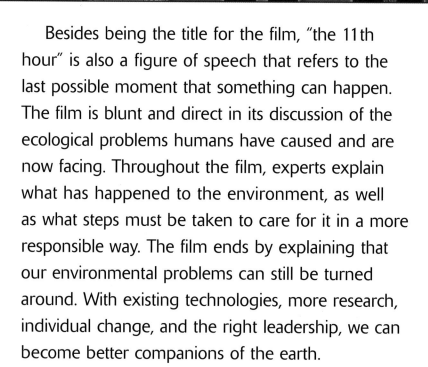

Besides being the title for the film, "the 11th hour" is also a figure of speech that refers to the last possible moment that something can happen. The film is blunt and direct in its discussion of the ecological problems humans have caused and are now facing. Throughout the film, experts explain what has happened to the environment, as well as what steps must be taken to care for it in a more responsible way. The film ends by explaining that our environmental problems can still be turned around. With existing technologies, more research, individual change, and the right leadership, we can become better companions of the earth.

What the Experts Say

Leonardo DiCaprio will be the first to tell you that he is not an expert on the environment. He has, however, surrounded himself with many knowledge-able people who are experts. *The 11th Hour* asks some basic but important questions about the future and enlists the help of fifty-four experts to answer those questions.

What do the experts in the film have to say? World-famous cosmologist Stephen Hawking comments,

Nadia Conners *(left)* and Leila Conners Petersen codirected DiCaprio's feature documentary, *The 11th Hour*. The sisters attended the film's premiere on August 8, 2007, in Los Angeles, California.

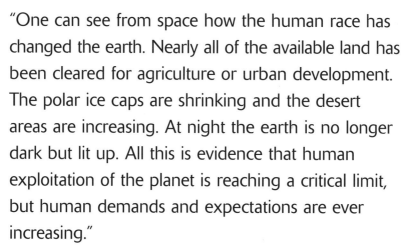

"One can see from space how the human race has changed the earth. Nearly all of the available land has been cleared for agriculture or urban development. The polar ice caps are shrinking and the desert areas are increasing. At night the earth is no longer dark but lit up. All this is evidence that human exploitation of the planet is reaching a critical limit, but human demands and expectations are ever increasing."

Environmentalist and entrepreneur Paul Hawken warns, "The problem that confronts us is that every living system in the biosphere is in decline and the rate of decline is accelerating. There isn't one peer-reviewed scientific article that's been published in the last twenty years that contradicts that statement. Living systems are coral reefs. They're our climatic stability, forest cover, the oceans themselves, aquifers, water, the conditions of the soil, biodiversity. They go on and on as they get more specific. But the fact is, there isn't one living system that is stable or is improving. And those living systems provide the basis for all life."

Businessman and broadcaster Thom Hartmann adds his own comments during the film: "Some

people suggest that in order to live sustainably, we have to go out into the woods and put on animal skins and live on roots and berries. And the simple reality is that we do have technology. The question is, how can we use our understanding of science and our understanding of technology along with our understanding of culture, and how culture changes, to create a culture that will interact with science and with the world around us in a sustainable fashion?"

DiCaprio concludes, "So, we find ourselves on the brink. It's clear humans have had a devastating impact on our planet's ecological web of life. Because we've waited, because we've turned our backs on nature's warning signs, and because our political and corporate leaders have consistently ignored the overwhelming scientific evidence, the challenges we face are that much more difficult. We are in the environmental age whether we like it or not. So, what does the future look like? We know the United States, the greatest consumer and source of waste, needs to make a transition to a greener future, but will our pivotal generation create a sustainable world in time? What will guide this massive change? And does nature hold the answers we need to help

This movie poster promotes *The 11th Hour*, the environmental film that DiCaprio produced and narrated. The documentary opened in theaters during the summer of 2007.

restore our planet's resources, protect our atmosphere, and therefore help all life survive?"

The Filmmakers

Leila Conners Petersen and Nadia Conners, who coproduced and codirected *The 11th Hour*, founded the Tree Media Group to produce film projects. Tree Media's Web site says of its mission, "Media has the power to change the world: it shares our stories, it drives culture, it shapes our lives. Tree Media Group is a production company with a mission to use media to support and sustain civil society while promoting peace through understanding."

Over the past decade, Tree Media Group has produced projects about global transformation, conflict resolution, the environment, and various progressive movements. The Tree Media Group has produced other Internet films besides *Global Warning* and *Water Planet*. Two of them are *Thoughts from Within*, a short film with a personal poem by Woody Harrelson, and *Healthy Oceans, Healthy Humans*, a short film narrated by Meryl Streep, which explains how all life on the earth is dependent on the oceans. Some of the films can be

Making a Green Movie

Making films tends to be very costly. In fact, *Titanic*, the movie that made DiCaprio a star, was one of the most expensive films ever made. Major films often run over budget, and the cost associated with producing even a simple film usually runs into the millions of dollars.

While creating *The 11th Hour*, a film whose message is a call for environmental change, the production team tried to operate as an example of the environmentalist message the film promotes. In fact, the film's credits end with the line, "Every effort has been made to reduce the environmental impact in the making of this film."

What did the producers do to minimize their carbon footprint? First, the carbon emissions that were created during the making of the film were offset by an investment made toward renewable energy sources. Also, the film crew was kept to a small number, and they managed to interview more than seventy experts in a very short time. Rather than going to each location to film each expert individually, the crew often traveled to conferences that many of the scientists were already attending. By doing this and by performing the interviews over short periods at the conferences, they limited both their air and ground transportation,

thereby cutting down on the carbon footprint of everyone involved.

In addition, the film producers used stock footage whenever possible and eschewed shooting new footage, which creates extra carbon waste. And finally, they recycled, reused set props and backdrops, and used hybrid vehicles to minimize waste and environmental impact.

Titanic, the film that made DiCaprio famous, was not a "green" movie. This massive model of the real *Titanic* contributed to the film's $200 million cost, making it one of the most expensive films ever made.

viewed on the Tree Media Group Web site (http://
www.treemedia.com).

After the New York premiere of *The 11th Hour*,
on August 10, 2007, Nadia Conners and Leila
Conners Petersen were interviewed along with
DiCaprio on ABC's *Nightline*. About the film, Nadia
said, "What we tried to do was create a story about
humanity, and the planet, and how we got here,
why we're here, why we're stuck here and how we
can get out of this situation." When asked if these
environmental problems still need to be explained
to people, she responded, "Yes. I mean, completely.
The main reason is because the response isn't there.
This needs to be a major societal change and it's not
happening."

Leila Conners Petersen added, "I think we want
them to walk away from the film saying, 'OK, I get
it, there is a problem.' But what's so amazing and
exciting about the time we live in is that there are
solutions. The solutions are there."

The interviewer then presented the women with
the question many shoppers are asked when bagging
their groceries: paper or plastic? No strangers to the

environmental concept of recycled products and waste reduction, both sisters responded, "Neither. Bring your own bag!"

Sustainable Design

"Sustainable design" is a term used to describe ways to create things without either harming the environment or using nonrenewable resources.

This community in England, the Beddington Zero Energy Development (BedZED), is an example of sustainable design. It was built to be carbon-neutral, meaning it produces all the energy it consumes.

With sustainable design, buildings, objects, and human-made landscaping serve their necessary functions, but at the same time, they have little or no negative impact on the natural world around them. In fact, some positive impact may even be achieved in the process. From small, everyday objects to large multistory buildings, many things can be made using sustainable design.

Featured in *The 11th Hour* is William McDonough, one the world's leading experts on sustainable design. McDonough tells how he was hired to help redesign Ford's River Rouge factory, in Dearborn, Michigan. An explosion in 1999 had destroyed the original plant. Today, after the redesign, it is one of the most eco-friendly car production plants ever built. The roof of the building is covered with a plant called sedum, which insulates the building while also making use of excess rain runoff. The building also has skylights that cut down on electricity used to light the factory.

McDonough has been a pioneer in the field of eco-friendly architecture as well as recycling almost since their inception. He has won numerous awards

and has been written up in *Time* magazine and the *New York Times*. He is also profiled on the movie's accompanying Web site, http://www.11thhouraction. com. McDonough's interview from the film is featured on the Web site. In it, he talks about his approach to sustainable design: "If we think about the tree as a design, it's something that makes oxygen, sequesters carbon, fixes nitrogen, distills water, provides a habitat for hundreds of species, accrues solar energy, makes complex sugars and food, creates microclimates, self replicates. So, what would it be like to design a building like a tree? What would it be like to design a city like a forest? So what would a building be like if it were photosynthetic? What if it took solar energy and converted it to productive and delightful use?"

As the future unfolds, innovative thinkers like William McDonough will help sustainable designers change the way our society builds—and the way we live.

Message of Hope

The 11th Hour is a film with a strong warning and a tough message from the experts: The direction we

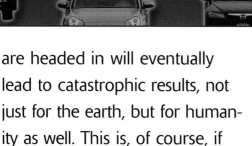
are headed in will eventually lead to catastrophic results, not just for the earth, but for humanity as well. This is, of course, if change does not happen soon.

However, as with DiCaprio's Web shorts, *Global Warning* and *Water Planet*, *The 11th Hour* ends on a positive, hopeful note. The final word given by the film is that all is not lost. Making changes, embracing new technologies, buying eco-friendly products, voting for government officials who care about the environment, and getting personally educated and involved are all mentioned as possible ways we can create a better future.

The 11th Hour explains that the power to change is essentially

Leonardo DiCaprio poses next to a movie poster at the Los Angeles opening of *The 11th Hour*. The film represents a different kind of starring role for the actor.

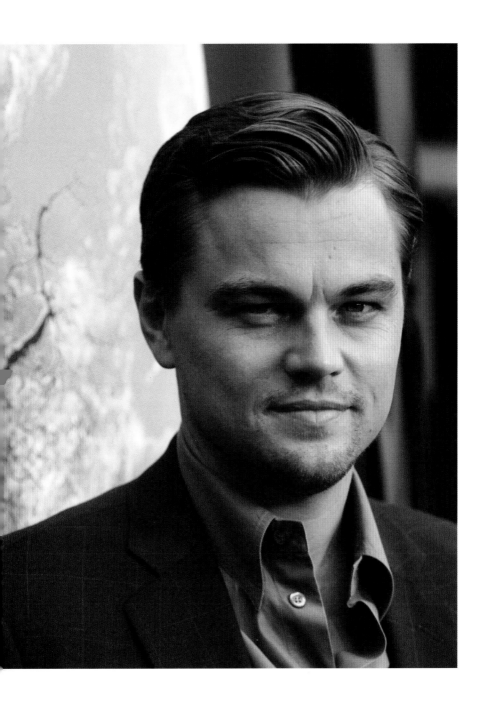

in the viewer's hands. Small changes by individuals, the film contends, will collectively reverse the effects of decades of irresponsible behavior. Small personal changes in consumption will also lead to larger corporate changes, as companies see what people want and move in the direction that is best for business—and the environment.

CHAPTER FIVE

The Future Is Now

Now is the time for environmental change. Each of us is merely one individual person, but together, we make up neighborhoods, local communities, towns, large cities, and huge societies. Collectively, we create a vast and powerful human web made up of billions. If we change our behavior together, great things can happen quickly. If we don't collectively alter our behavior, our current lifestyles will have catastrophic and irreversible results, not only for humanity but also for the earth's ecosystems and the multitudes of plants and animals that share the planet with us.

The Future of Environmentalism

At the end of *The 11th Hour,* Leonardo DiCaprio sums up the film's message: "Environmentalism was once the project of a passionate few. Now millions of people have responded to ecological destruction and have created the groundwork for a sustainable and just world. With the onset of global warming and other catastrophic events, environmentalism has

DiCaprio's environmental efforts set an example for his many fans. He appears here on the set of his documentary *The 11th Hour.*

become today a broader unifying human issue. We as citizens, leaders, consumers, and voters have the opportunity to help integrate ecology into governmental policy and everyday living standards. During this critical period of human history, healing the damage of industrial civilization is the task of our generation. Our response depends on the conscious evolution of our species, and this response could very well save this unique blue planet for future generations."

The possibility for change lies with us, with our understanding of the ecology-related problems the world now faces. We have the knowledge, and as a result of the damage and mistakes we have made, we have the hindsight to know that changes are necessary. According to the experts, the changes won't be easy, but together it should be a very promising time to be alive, provided we all lend a hand.

In the film *The 11th Hour*, Paul Hawken says, "The great thing about the dilemma we're in is that we get to reimagine every single thing we do. In other words, there isn't one single thing that we make that doesn't require a complete remake. And so there are two ways of looking at that. One is like,

'Oh my gosh, what a big burden.' The other way to look at it, which is the way I prefer, is, 'What a great time to be born! What a great time to be alive!' Because this generation gets to essentially completely change this world."

What You Can Do

Sometimes, change can be hard. Many people lack the means to restructure their houses and have solar power installed, or to buy a hybrid car. There are, however, simple solutions out there for everyone, regardless of economic background, geographical location, or lifestyle.

Putting many of these solutions into effect would take little or no extra time out of our already busy lives. Some simple steps include using less energy in your home. The average home in the United States uses the energy equivalent of 1,253 gallons of oil each year. Turning off lights when they are not being used and using less heat or air conditioning when possible are ways to use less energy every day. Using washers, dryers, and dishwashers can account for about 25 percent of a home's energy use. Running these appliances only when they are

full can help to cut down on wasted electricity and energy used to heat water.

These are just a few of the simple steps we can each take to reduce our reliance on fossil fuels and reduce waste in general.

Casting Your Vote

As *The 11th Hour* makes clear, we have a chance to "cast our vote" with every purchase we make. What does that mean? When you go to the store and buy a product made by a company that operates with sustainable, eco-friendly methods, you are making it known that you approve of that company and its practices. You are choosing, or "voting for," that company over the others that produce similar items. If everyone were to shop with this purpose, the companies that make the most eco-friendly products and operate in the most eco-friendly manner would make more profits. The profits of other companies would suffer as a result, and these other companies would have to change their ways in order to survive in the marketplace.

For example, everyone uses lightbulbs in their homes. When you are shopping for lightbulbs, the

store shelves offer many choices. Choosing compact fluorescent bulbs that cut down on energy use and last longer than conventional bulbs will send an environmental message to the producers. By choosing a product more in harmony with the earth's environment, you cast a vote that says this type of product is worth making.

You can also choose to buy recycled paper or choose to buy products made of plastics that can be recycled. As more and more consumers cast their individual votes, companies will get a strong collective message, and they will begin offering more of these earth-friendly

It's getting easier for consumers to make choices that help the environment. Many communities now have stores carrying compact fluorescent lightbulbs.

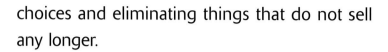
choices and eliminating things that do not sell any longer.

Changes at School

You go to school every day, but have you ever thought about how eco-friendly your school is? Look around your classrooms for recycling bins. Let your teachers and classmates know that seventeen trees are saved for each ton of paper recycled. (Americans use close to ninety million tons of paper each year.) Check out your school cafeteria, too. Americans use about 2.5 million plastic bottles each hour! Recycling steel, tin, aluminum, plastic, and glass helps cut down on waste to make a more eco-friendly school.

Check to see that lights are shut off in rooms that are not being used. If this policy is not practiced at your school, talk to your teacher or someone else who can help change the way things are done. Bringing environmental awareness to schools helps spread the word to all of your fellow students. They, in turn, will bring the message into their own homes.

Corporate Help

The responsibility for change does not lie only with individuals. Corporations and industries can speed up the pace of sweeping changes. They can quickly eliminate old, outdated technologies, while introducing new, cleaner, and more eco-friendly practices. If just one large factory reduced or eliminated its carbon emissions, it could equal the efforts of thousands of eco-conscious individuals.

Businessman and industrial engineer Ray Anderson says in *The 11th Hour*, "I think the industrial system has to be reinvented. Today the throughput of the industrial system, from mine and wellhead to finished product, ends up in a landfill or incinerator. For every truckload of product with lasting value, thirty-two truckloads of waste are produced. That's mind-boggling, but it's true. So we have a system that is a waste-making system. And clearly we cannot continue to dig up the earth and turn it to waste."

It is not an easy task for corporations to change to alternative energy sources. The switch will be costly. A big corporation may have thousands of buildings that will need to have heating, lighting, or electrical systems changed. For older buildings, at the time they were built, fossil fuels were the only choice. Making changes to these structures would be difficult in the short-term. But the cost of not making these changes is even greater in the long run.

How can individuals find out more about the companies whose products they buy? Writing letters to companies asking what they are doing to reduce their carbon footprints is a good place to start. Educating ourselves about the practices of different corporations can help us make consumer decisions regarding which companies we want to give our money to when we shop or pay for services. As Leonardo DiCaprio reminds us in his films and on his Web site, informed and responsible consumers can force companies to make the changes we need.

Companies in more developed countries like the United States have the biggest changes to make. Companies in developing countries, on the other hand, may not need much pressure to switch over to greener technologies. They have a better opportunity to use newer technologies right away because they

Rethinking a Whole Town

As an environmental champion, Leonardo DiCaprio may have accomplished a lot already. But from the looks of his next project, he may have just been getting warmed up.

On May 4, 2007, a tornado hit the town of Greensburg, Kansas, virtually wiping it off the map. After seeing the destruction caused by the tornado, DiCaprio had the idea to rebuild the town as an "Eco-Town." Along with Craig Piligian, of Pilgrim Films & Television, DiCaprio brought his idea to the Discovery Channel, whose producers liked the idea. Soon, Discovery Communications president and CEO David Zaslav announced that they would rebuild the town as an eco-friendly model of sustainability. The project would become a thirteen-episode series called Eco-Town, which would air on Discovery's new channel, Planet Green.

DiCaprio is executive producer of the show with his company, Appian Way. Discovery's Planet Green and Craig Piligian also provide additional resources. The town of Greensburg itself and the governor of Kansas, too, have input into the direction the project takes. Once again, DiCaprio has succeeded in using his celebrity status to get out the message that changes need to happen now.

This is Greensburg, Kansas, following the devastating tornado in 2007. DiCaprio and the Discovery Channel hope to rebuild Greensburg as a model of sustainable design.

can be incorporated into the buildings and infra-structure now, as these countries are being developed.

Governmental Help

One important way the government can help to make improvements in our broken system is to make new laws. We already know that laws can bring about changes that help the environment and

improve human health. In the 1960s, for example, water quality in many areas of the United States and Canada was poor. Many rivers were too dirty to swim in, and a lot of people became sick and even died from drinking polluted tap water. Action had to be taken. The Clean Water Act of the 1970s helped to lessen water pollution and regulate the quality of water we drink and use in our daily lives. Because of the laws, systems were put in place, rules were followed, and improvements were made.

We have also seen evidence of helpful laws that protect threatened species. Laws against hunting protected animals have helped keep endangered species from passing into extinction. The same kinds of laws need to be made regarding carbon emissions and alternative energy sources. Voting for leaders who support alternative energy, reward carbon emission reduction, and make laws that protect the environment is a good way to steer our way toward a greener, better future.

In Conclusion

Through the great efforts of scientists, researchers, conscientious regular people everywhere, and

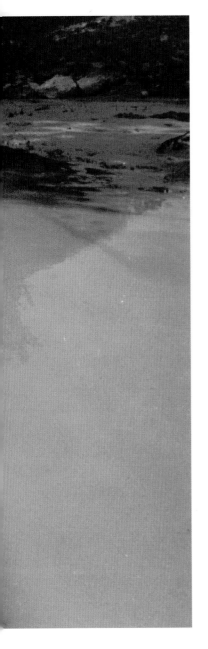

celebrity environmentalists like Leonardo DiCaprio, more people are coming to understand the importance of environmental protection and awareness. At this time, in addition to making changes ourselves, we must demand change from our civic leaders. When we have leaders who believe strongly in something, change can happen quickly.

R. James Woolsey, former director of the Central Intelligence Agency, summarized this point well in *The 11th Hour*. He said about the difficult times during World War II, "This country can move awfully fast, if it wants to. Keep in mind that after December 7, 1941, Roosevelt

This photo from the early 1970s shows the effects of water pollution in New York's Hudson River. This thick industrial waste and sewage threatened fish and humans alike.

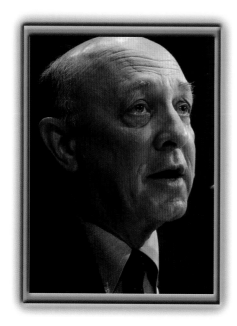

R. James Woolsey is the former director of the CIA. He speaks in *The 11th Hour* about the environmental strides that are possible with help from government officials.

went to Jimmy Byrnes and said, 'You're my deputy president for mobilizing the economy. Anybody crosses you, they cross me.' Within six months, Detroit was completely retooled, not making cars anymore, making military trucks, tanks, fighter aircraft, and in three years and eight months from the beginning of that war, we had mobilized, and had defeated imperial Japan, Fascist Italy, Nazi Germany, together with the British and other allies, and had begun demobilization. Three years and eight months."

Imagine the changes that could take place if leaders were that passionate about the environment.

GLOSSARY

abstract Theoretical, or not sufficiently factual or concrete.

alternative energy Source of energy that is environmentally sound and not in the mainstream, such as wind or solar energy.

atmosphere The mass of air surrounding the earth's surface.

biodiversity Variety of life and species on our planet.

bioregion Land and water territory whose limits are defined by biological and ecological systems.

carbon dioxide Gas naturally present in the atmosphere.

carbon footprint Representation of the amount of greenhouse gases produced by human activity.

carbon sequestration Capture and long-term storage of carbon in forests, soils, and the oceans.

catastrophic Related to a momentous, violent event that happens quickly.

computer model Program or system that uses a built-in set of rules to predict the results of a process or to simulate how a given set of conditions will play out.

consensus Group agreement.

contradictory Opposite; implying that another statement is untrue.

disenchanted Dissatisfied or disappointed.

ecosystem Community of interacting organisms and their environment.

entrepreneur One who assumes the risks to start a business.

eschew To shun or avoid.

exploit To use unjustly.

fossil fuels Natural fuels—including coal, oil, and natural gas—formed by remains of living organisms.

global warming Gradual increase in the overall temperature of the earth's lower atmosphere.

greenhouse effect Trapping of the sun's warmth in the atmosphere.

hybrid vehicle Vehicle that uses at least two different technologies to make the vehicle run, such as a gasoline engine and an electric motor.

idyllic Picturesque and naturally pleasing.

Industrial Revolution Period in the late eighteenth and early nineteenth centuries of rapid development of industry caused by the introduction of machinery.

infrastructure Underlying resources of a community that allow for transportation and communication.

nonprofit Business whose purpose is to serve a cause rather than make money.

nonrenewable resource Natural material that is considered limited because of the long time it takes for it to form.

obscure Mysterious or hidden.

photosynthetic Describing plants able to convert light to energy.

renewable resource Resource that will not run out because it is produced quickly, through natural means.

solar panels Arrangement of solar cells that convert the sun's energy to electricity.

sustainability Ability to provide for a population without negative environmental effects.

symbiotic Describing a relationship between two different organisms that mutually benefit from the relationship.

trifling Without serious purpose.

utopian Having ideal, and usually impractical, social conditions.

FOR MORE INFORMATION

Canadian Environmental Assessment Agency
22nd Floor, Place Bell
160 Elgin Street
Ottawa, ON K1A 0H3
Canada
(613) 957-0700
E-mail: info@ceaa-acee.gc.ca
Web site: http://www.ceaa-acee.gc.ca
This agency provides assessments of the environment
that help people make informed decisions about
sustainable development.

Clean Air Watch
1250 Connecticut Avenue NW, Suite 200
Washington, DC 20036
(202) 558-3527
Web site: http://www.cleanairwatch.org
Clean Air Watch is a national nonprofit organization
for protecting laws and policies regarding clean
air throughout the United States.

Environmental Protection Agency (EPA)
1200 Pennsylvania Avenue NW
Washington, DC 20460
(800) 424-4372
Web site: http://www.epa.gov
The EPA is dedicated to protecting the environment of the United States. It also collects
information about climate change and greenhouse gas emissions.

Environment Canada
Inquiry Centre
70 Cremazie Street
Gatineau, QC K1A 0H3
Canada
(800) 668-6767
E-mail: enviroinfo@ec.gc.ca
Web site: http://www.ec.gc.ca
Environment Canada is the department of the
Canadian government responsible for issuing
weather forecasts and warnings and monitoring
Canada's environmental policies.

Global Green USA
2218 Main Street, 2nd Floor
Santa Monica, CA 90405
(310) 581-2700
E-mail: ggusa@globalgreen.org
Web site: http://www.globalgreen.org
Global Green is an environmental organization
   addressing climate change and safe drinking water.

Natural Resources Defense Council
40 West 20th Street
New York, NY 10011
(212) 727-2700
E-mail: nrdcinfo@nrdc.org
Web site: http://www.nrdc.org
This environmental action agency works to protect
   wildlife, wilderness areas, and clean air and water.

The Student Conservation Association
689 River Road
P.O. Box 550
Charlestown, NH 03603-0550

(603) 543-1700

E-mail: AskUs@thesca.org

Web site: http://www.thesca.org

This nonprofit organization offers conservation programs and internships to students, including high school students.

Web Sites

Due to the changing nature of Internet links, Rosen Publishing has developed an online list of Web sites related to the subject of this book. This site is updated regularly. Please use this link to access the list:

http://www.rosenlinks.com/cea/ledi

Benyus, Janine M. *Biomimicry: Innovation Inspired by Nature.* New York, NY: Harper Perennial, 2002.

Gore, Al. *The Assault on Reason.* New York, NY: Penguin Press, 2007.

Gore, Al. *Earth in the Balance: Ecology and the Human Spirit.* New York, NY: Rodale Books, 2006.

Gore, Al. *An Inconvenient Truth.* New York, NY: Rodale Books, 2006.

Hartmann, Thom. *Before It's Too Late.* New York, NY: Three Rivers Press, 2004.

Hartmann, Thom. *The Last Hours of Ancient Sunlight: The Fate of the World and What We Can Do.* New York, NY: Three Rivers Press, 2004.

Hill, Julia. *One Makes the Difference: Inspiring Actions That Change Our World.* New York, NY: HarperOne, 2002.

McDonough, William. *Cradle to Cradle: Remaking the Way We Make Things.* New York, NY: North Point Press, 2002.

McKibben, Bill. *Fight Global Warming Now: Your Handbook for Taking Action in Your Community.* New York, NY: Henry Holt and Company, 2007.

BIBLIOGRAPHY

Alberta Government. "Surface Water Quality."
Retrieved October 7, 2007 (http://www3.gov.
ab.ca/env/water/SWQ/index.cfm).

Amtrak.com. "What Is a Carbon Footprint?" Retrieved
August 8, 2007 (http://www.amtrak.com/servlet/
Satellite?c=WSArticlePage&cid=117337644452&
pagename=WhistleStop/WSArticlePage/Blank_
Template).

Armour, Terry. "DiCaprio Takes on Bigger Role:
Environmentalist." *Chicago Tribune*. August 19,
2007. Retrieved August 20, 2007 (http://
metromix.chicagotribune.com).

Attenborough, David. *Life on Earth*. New York, NY:
Little, Brown, 1979.

Bakhsian, Sara Shereen. "Leonardo DiCaprio's
'11th Hour.'" Beliefnet. Retrieved August 20,
2007 (http://www.beliefnet.com/story/223/
story/22304_1.html).

BBC News. "DiCaprio Tries to Calm Beach Storm."
January 18, 1999. Retrieved August 26, 2007
(http://news.bbc.co.uk/2/hi/entertainment/
257354.stm).

Rutenberg, Jim. "A Knack for Controversy Worries ABC News." *New York Times*, April 10, 2000.

Sandell, Clayton. "Reducing Your Carbon Footprint." ABC News. June 7, 2006. Retrieved August 15, 2007 (http://abcnews.go.com/print?id=2049304).

The 79th Academy Awards. ABC television network. February 25, 2007.

Solomon, Deborah. "The Way We Live Now: 5-20-07: Questions for William McDonough; Calling Mr. Green." *New York Times*, May 20, 2007.

Time.com "Star Power Lights the Way." April 26, 2000. Retrieved August 22, 2007 (http://www.time.com/time/printout/0,8816,996754,00.html).

Tourtellotte, Bob. "DiCaprio Talks About Going Green and '11th Hour.'" August 16, 2007. Retrieved August 20, 2007 (http://www.canada.com/components).

Tree Media Group. "Who We Are." Retrieved September 10, 2007 (http://www.treemedia.com/press/index.html).

INDEX

About the Authors

Kathy and Adam Furgang also wrote about environmental issues in *On the Move: Green Transportation*, a book in Rosen Central's Your Carbon Footprint series. The couple lives near Albany, New York, with their two young sons. For ten years, Kathy Furgang has been a writer and editor of science books and textbooks for both students and teachers. The many topics she has written about include conservation, recycling, biodiversity, and renewable energy.

Photo Credits

Cover, p. 1 (background, portrait), pp. 5, 20–21, 25, 34, 65, 94 © Getty Images; cover, p. 1 (top right), p. 31 © AFP/Getty Images; p. 13 © Aurora/Getty Images; p. 28 © Paramount Classics/courtesy Everett Collection; p. 40 © Laura Parr/ZUMA/Corbis; p. 46 © Fred Prouser/Reuters/Corbis; pp. 54–55 © National Geographic/Getty Images; pp. 58, 71, 84–85, 90, 92–93 © AP Photos; pp. 62–63 © Wireimage/Getty Images; p. 68 © Warner Independent Pictures/ Photofest; p. 73 © Ashley Cooper/Corbis; pp. 76–77 © Mario Anzuoni/Reuters/Corbis; p. 80 © Warner Independent Pictures/ Courtesy Everett Collection.

Designer: Tahara Anderson; Editor: Christopher Roberts
Photo Researcher: Marty Levick